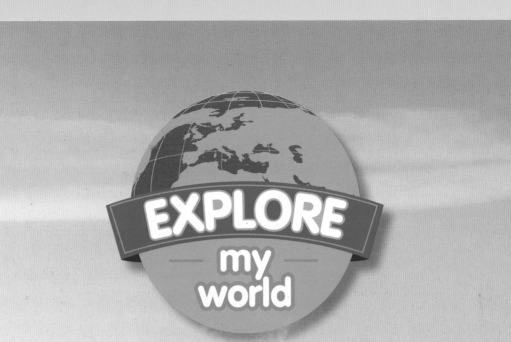

A Tree Grows Up

Marfé Ferguson Delano

NATIONAL
GEOGRAPHIC
KiDS

WASHINGTON, D.C.

Look!

What's that squirrel eating? It's an acorn. Squirrels love to munch on crunchy acorns.

Acorns drop from oak trees in the fall. Squirrels eat many of them. But they don't eat them all.

The squirrels
missed this acorn.
One by one, falling leaves
cover it. The wind blows
soil over it. In winter,
snowflakes blanket the
acorn in white.

Sprout!

When spring comes, the shell of the acorn splits open. A tiny root peeks out and pokes down into the soil.

Soon a little green stem with little leaves pushes up and reaches toward the sun. It's a baby oak tree.

Day by day, the baby tree grows. Its stem, called a trunk, becomes harder. By the end of the summer, it's as tall as a pencil.

Year by year, the young tree grows. When it's five years old, it's tall enough for people to stand under. Songbirds perch on its slim branches. *Chirp, chirrup!*

Just like you, a tree needs food to live and grow. But a tree can make its own food!

Sunshine helps the leaves turn air and water into a sugary food. This food flows through the veins in the leaves to every part of the tree.

Every fall, when the weather turns chilly, the tree's leaves stop making food. They change from green to red to brown. Then they dry up and fall off.

Brrrr!

In winter, the tree looks dead, but it's not. It's just resting. It rests all winter long.

Spring brings rain and warm sunshine. The oak tree wakes up. New leaves spread wide to catch the sunlight.

The tree keeps growing taller and taller. Its trunk and branches grow thicker and thicker. Squirrels scurry up and down the trunk. A family of birds nests on a branch.

Bloom!

One spring, when the oak tree is about 30 years old, *surprise!* Small flowers grow next to the new leaves.

After a few weeks, the flowers fall off. Little knobs form where the flowers used to be. They are baby acorns! Over the summer, they get bigger and bigger.

In the fall, the acorns drop from the tree. Many animals come to feed on the fallen acorns: chipmunks, wild turkeys, bears, blue jays, deer— and squirrels, of course!

So Big!

The oak is now a grown-up tree. It will keep making acorns for the rest of its long life. It will keep growing taller. Its trunk and branches will grow thicker and thicker. One day a branch will be strong enough for a swing. *Whee!*

Up, Out, and Down

A tree gets bigger in three ways. It grows up, it grows out, and it grows down.

The top of a tree is called the crown. It's made up of branches and twigs.

Tiny tubes inside the tree trunk carry water from the roots to the leaves.

Roots hold a tree in place. They keep it from falling over when strong winds blow.

Growing Up: Every year, new shoots push out of the buds at the tips of branches and twigs. This causes the twigs to grow longer—and the tree to grow taller.

1

Growing Out: Every year, a new layer of wood forms underneath the bark of the trunk and branches. This makes the trunk and branches get thicker.

2

Growing Down: Most of a tree's roots are underground. Every year, the roots spread wider and deeper. That's how the tree grows down.

3

downy woodpecker

Home Sweet Tree

honeybee

Birds and squirrels aren't the only animals that make their home in oak trees. Here are just a few of the many different animals that live in oaks.

white-footed mouse

What animals have you seen in oaks or other trees near your home?

tree cricket

mourning cloak butterfly

gray tree frog

skunk

Super Seeds

oak tree

Most trees begin their lives as seeds. Seeds come in many different shapes and sizes. An acorn is a seed. It grows into an oak tree. Acorns have a smooth, hard shell with a rough, bumpy cap.

acorn

maple tree

maple seed

Here are some other kinds
of seeds. How many of them
have you seen?

cherry tree

pine tree

pinecone seed

cherry seed

apple tree

apple seed

Leaf Rubbings

Collect leaves in different shapes and sizes.

Place a leaf on a hard, flat surface, with the bottom side of the leaf facing up.

3

Put a piece of thin paper over the leaf.

4

Gently rub the side of a crayon back and forth on the part of the paper over the leaf. Be sure to rub over the entire leaf.

5

There you have it— lovely leaf art!

For Everett Delano Gunderman with love from his Aunt Marfé

Since 1888, the National Geographic Society has funded more than
12,000 research, exploration, and preservation projects around the
world. The Society receives funds from National Geographic Partners,
LLC, funded in part by your purchase. A portion of the proceeds from this
book supports this vital work. To learn more, visit www.natgeo.com/info.

NATIONAL GEOGRAPHIC and Yellow Border Design are trademarks of
the National Geographic Society, used under license.

National Geographic supports K–12 educators with
ELA Common Core Resources. Visit www.natgeoed.org/
commoncore for more information.

Trade paperback ISBN: 978-1-4263-2429-1
Reinforced library binding ISBN: 978-1-4263-2430-7

The publisher gratefully acknowledges Dr. Gary D. Coleman
of the University of Maryland's Plant Sciences department and
early childhood development specialist Catherine Hughes for
their expert review of this book.

Art director and designer: Amanda Larsen

Printed in Hong Kong
16/THK/1